The Heart of an Entrepreneur

A JOURNEY THROUGH TIME

KELVIN K. LUCAS

HIS GLORY CREATIONS PUBLISHING, LLC
WENDELL

His Glory Creations Publishing, LLC
Wendell, North Carolina

Copyright © 2021 by Kelvin K. Lucas

ISBN: 978-1-950861-19-4

DEDICATION

———————

To those aspiring to serve the needs of humanity with:
compassion, integrity and humility!

***And he said unto them, "How is it that ye sought me?
wist ye not that I must be about my Father's
business?"***

Luke 2:49

CONTENTS

The Heart of an Entrepreneur

A JOURNEY THROUGH TIME

As you read the book, I will share with you some of my personal experiences as an entrepreneur during a segment entitled, "**Heart 2 ♡ !**".

I welcome you to reflect upon your own life experiences in the "**My ↪ Turn!**" segment. These are designed for you to engage in thought provoking moments that may help you recognize the treasure the Lord has given to you to maximize for his glory!

ACKNOWLEDGMENTS

I want to thank the Take It By Force Ministries, Inc.
Board of Directors, volunteers and local businesses that
have supported our ministry efforts since 2001!

The Heart of an Entrepreneur

A JOURNEY THROUGH TIME

1

The Businessman

When you think of the ultimate entrepreneur, Jesus Christ, should be at the top of your list. He was the most successful business person in the history of mankind. He: set the benchmark for strategic planning, operated at a low overhead cost, understood what his mission statement was, and had a clear vision as to how to accomplish it. He even had a board of directors whom he handpicked and trained himself. No other entrepreneur can even come close to the trailblazing example Christ has given to the marketplace.

Perhaps the most important lesson to learn from studying the ministry of Christ is his heart's desire to do what was pleasing to God the Father. In the Gospel of Luke 2:42-46, it records an episode when Jesus, as a middle school-aged youth, was visiting Jerusalem with his parents, Joseph and Mary. When it was time to return home, they could not find Jesus. They thought that he had gone to stay with relatives, but actually, Jesus took the initiative to engage himself in conversations with the doctors and other leaders in the temple to get a feel for the environment.

******Heart 2**♡! – *Sometimes you must be willing to approach those who have a higher status than you do. I remember back in 2001, when I met with the Mayor of my hometown to discuss the idea of hosting our first camp meeting event at an area park. I scheduled the meeting shortly after the Parks and Recreation Director declined our proposal. Since the initial pencil sketch, I drew while attending a financial workshop, I knew the vision that the Lord had given me regarding the camp meeting event, so I could not allow an initial no to be the end of the matter. The meeting with the Mayor went extremely well, and we were well on our way to a collaboration with the Assistant City Manager along with the parks and recreation department, that has spanned for 20 years. Since 2002, Take It By Force Ministries, Inc. has conducted 30 camp meeting events in local parks. Great things can happen when you network with the right people!*

Now, of course, Joseph and Mary were concerned about Jesus, and when they confronted him concerning his whereabouts, Jesus said unto them, "How is it that ye sought me?... I must be about my Father's business." He understood the value of time and sought to maximize his opportunity to network on the stage he would soon transform. Jesus was a businessman! He displayed the heart of a true entrepreneur: a heart that knows what the need of the marketplace is, and takes into consideration, God's will to meet that need.

Well, what is **God's will**? I'm glad you asked. I will talk more about that later on. But for now, understand the heart of a true entrepreneur comprehends that God is the compass, and Christ is the map which your life journey should follow. God is the governing force behind the scenes that supplies what is needed.

Psalm 24:1-2 declares, "The earth is the Lord's, and the fulness thereof; the world, and they that dwell therein..." He has the resources available to assist you with your vision at the time when you need them! Those resources are not just limited to monetary, but he enables you to cross paths with individuals who can release tangible as well as intangible goods into your life and business establishment.

****Heart 2♡! – *I remember when I was 15 years old. During the summer of 1989, I was invited to attend Bible camp at a local church. It was a wonderful experience that would change my life forever. Later that summer, I became a member of the church and, through the years: an Elder, Youth Pastor and Business Manager. It's worth noting that the Pastor of the church, Bishop Haywood Parker, served as a great mentor who taught me the fundamentals of non-profit management. The lessons that I learned laid the foundation for the success I enjoy as an entrepreneur TODAY! I encourage you to recognize mentoring opportunities and maximize them.*

God is also a supplier of material resources as well. I recall we were preparing for the first camp meeting at Branch Street Park. I was networking my brain out trying to secure: funding, cultural arts groups, donations, liability insurance, a 40x40 tent with chairs, and a port -a -john. It was an emotional roller coaster. We would always stay glued to the weather channel, hoping that it would not rain, but the Lord reminded us that we would be under a huge tent! Everything always came together.

Over the years, as we continued to facilitate the camp meetings, God has given us favor with local businesses that were willing to donate items as well as offer discounts. TIBF has been very fortunate to receive the support it needed to make a difference in the marketplace, even last-minute support. The week of an event we had coming up on a Saturday, the grant funding was delayed and not guaranteed to arrive on time. The budget was already tight, and our backs were against the wall. That Friday afternoon around 1:30 pm, the little white postal jeep pulled up in front of the mailbox. After checking the box daily, I was scared to go this time; but I knew I had to. So, I grabbed the mail out of the box and began sorting through the pile, only to find the grant check at the bottom! My eyes got really BIG. I jumped in my car and headed to the bank! That Sunday, we ran around the church, thanking the Lord for his provision, that was right on time!

****My ⟲ Turn! – Can you recall a mentoring experience that shaped your life? Talk about it below, and if possible, connect with your mentee and express a remark of gratitude. If they are no longer alive, thank God for the opportunity you had to cross paths! Also, reflect upon the provisions God has made in your entrepreneurial journey.

_____

_____

_____

_____

_____

$\mathcal{E}$ntrepreneurial $\mathcal{J}$ourney
through the years....

April 20, 2002
First Camp Meeting event at Branch St. Park
Rocky Mount, NC

June 15, 2002
Tom Stith Park
Rocky Mount, NC

Youth Tennis Clinic

Family Outreach

College Campus Ministry
NCWC-Rocky Mount, NC

"Learn more about God's Word in a very informal atmosphere designed to meet your needs!" Come and study...

" The Battle of the Wills"

?  ?

God's Way   vs.   My Way

Bible Study each Thursday from 7:30 pm-8:30 pm
NCWC Leon Russell Chapel
Beginning September 4, 2003

Founders:
Pastors Kelvin and Felicia Lucas

"Taking the Campus for Christ"
Sponsored by : Take It By Force Ministries Inc.
Mailing Address: P .O. Box 941~ Wendell, NC 27591
Phone: (919) 618-0260
Email: takeitbyforce@mybluelight.com

2003 Camp Meeting Events

Fire Safety Clinics

Original Board Members

The Heart of an Entrepreneur

A JOURNEY THROUGH TIME

2

You've Got to Figure it Out

As an entrepreneur you must: figure out what need(s) has God equipped you to meet; and utilize your life journey with: compassion, integrity, and humility to serve those needs. That's **God's will** and nobody did that better than Jesus!

So, what is an entrepreneur anyway? According to Webster's dictionary, an entrepreneur is one who: organizes, manages and carries the risk of operating a business. The risk includes the: ups, downs, known, unknown, problems, solutions and everything else between points A-Z. You must have the heart to: **ORGANIZE** *risk,* **MANAGE** *risk* and **CARRY** *risk.*

When you talk about being organized, one word that comes to mind is **order**. You must have some type of ordered structure in your life as an entrepreneur. Order can help you maximize time, think clearly and pursue your goals effectively. Jesus had an eye for proper order. In Matthew 4:19, as he began to choose his board of disciples, he made it quite clear what the goal was... "Follow me, and I will make you..." He was inviting them on a journey that would provide order while trying to enlarge the scope of their thinking.

A good example of this can be found in Luke 9:12-17 when Jesus challenged the disciples to feed the multitude (v. 13). Immediately, the disciples thought they needed to go and buy food (v. 13). Rather than wasting that time going to buy food, Jesus maximized time by identifying what was readily available to them. Sometimes in life, you must recognize what is available to you and make it work for you! I need to say that again, **"Sometimes in life, you need to recognize what is available to you and make it work for you!"** Jesus ordered the multitude to sit (v. 14), took what was available, looked up towards heaven, and gave God thanks (v. 16), which yielded a surplus. He went vertical on his board of disciples. Listen, you can't always focus on the horizontal: what's in front, beside or behind you. You've got to learn how to GO vertical. Look up to God and talk with him! That's what being an entrepreneur is about: taking your FAITH and your trade to the next level by allowing Christ to be your example! Now, of course, his board represented some level of risk, but he was willing to include them for the ride. Now that sounds familiar; even though we can engage in crazy decision making from time to time, God still keeps us onboard!

Secondly, an entrepreneur is one who manages. As a **manager,** you must be able to develop ideas, follow through with processes, and inspire yourself and others to achieve. This involves a certain level of delegation. Oftentimes as an entrepreneur, you are the only employee! You have got to make it happen. You're the only one in the room with the *Master's* plan. Can you effectively delegate to yourself what needs to be done and stay focused enough to finish it?

Check this out. In Luke 8: (41-42, 49-55) while Jesus was proceeding to go and heal Jairus's daughter, the report came that she had already died (v. 49). Jesus stuck with the process and inspired her father to do the same (v. 50). When Jesus arrived on the scene, he knew exactly what needed to happen: he took 3 disciples in with him (v. 51), told the crowd to be quiet and expressed his view concerning the matter (v. 52). While they laughed at him (v. 53), Jesus went inside and healed the young lady (vv. 54-55)! As a manager, you have to learn how to see things differently than everyone else, even if they laugh at you. It's called the BIGGER picture. While everyone is standing around wondering and looking, you go on in and get the job done!

When COVID-19 hit in 2020, I'm sure some were waiting to see if we would have our 31st camp meeting. They were waiting to see what would happen. I was determined to keep the ball rolling, and God did not allow external circumstances to hinder us. We were able to distribute school supplies to a local youth organization and hosted a successful virtual event with praise, worship and mime ministry.

****Heart 2♡! – *The best advice I can give you when it comes to self- delegation is: remain true to your focus. No matter what, manage life as it happens but always find your way back to the intended goal. Whether it's: planning a camp meeting, preparing a sermon, running the PTA, doing the laundry, reconciling the bank statements, helping with homework, paying bills, preparing dinner, mowing the lawn, planning the next date night or vacation, developing a marketing campaign, sitting in carpool, coaching little league, facilitating a workshop or Podcast, you have to find a routine and work it! Oh, I almost* *forgot, squeeze in a little ME time. Being a stay-at-home dad has taught me the importance of self-delegation, and I have been able to leverage that experience into my entrepreneurial journey! All things can and do work together!*

Jesus knew what he was supposed to do and the extent to which it needed to happen. In John 4:34, he said, "My meat is to do the will of him that sent me, and to finish his work." He understood the urgency behind processes and the necessity to get things done! That's why Jesus came. To inspire us as entrepreneurs to stick with the vision and get the job done! I always keep in mind, **"I can, I will, I did, let's do it again!"** That has been my entrepreneurial anthem for 20 years!

Thirdly, being an entrepreneur involves carrying the risk. When you **carry** something, it essentially becomes a part of you. It's similar to carrying your cross of purpose. Your cross is your contribution to the world! It includes the: **upswing, peak, downswing** and **valley** experiences.

The upswing consists of those times when things are looking good. The peak is when you are on top of it all. Reality kicks back in during the downswing as momentum dwindles only to regroup in the valley, and prepare for the next upswing. Such is life. You learn how to survive during the best and worst of times. How do you survive during the best of times? Resist the urge to become arrogant. Pride comes before the fall. Reduce the likelihood of the falling by remaining humble. How do you survive during the worst of times? Hang in there, and don't compromise the quality of what you offer. Serve the marketplace with integrity, regardless of where you are on the curve.

When you find yourself in the valley of the curve, use it as an opportunity to prepare for the upswing.

****Heart 2♡! – *When the TIBF grant funding program was discontinued in 2016, it challenged us to look for other resources. We were able to find a potential funding source, but the application required a social media page. Up to that point, I never really embraced social media, and our marketing was limited to: a three-ring binder, flyers and brochures. We were in a financial valley, but there was a marketing upswing on the horizon. The valley forced me to sit down and design a social media page that would serve two purposes: 1) Meet the grant qualification, 2) Revamp the marketing platform. Located in the financial valley were the building blocks for the next marketing phase!*

****My ↱Turn!** – Do you have a valley experience to reflect upon that has made a positive impact on your entrepreneurial journey?

_____

_____

_____

_____

_____

_____

_____

2004 Camp Meeting Events

Motivational Speaking

Community Vendors

2005 Camp Meeting Events

2006-2007 Camp Meeting Events

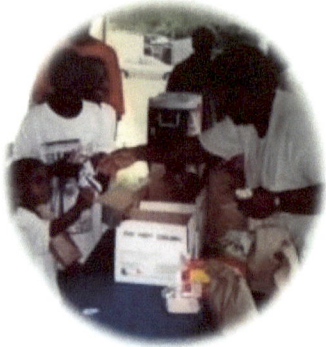

2008 Western Ave. Park

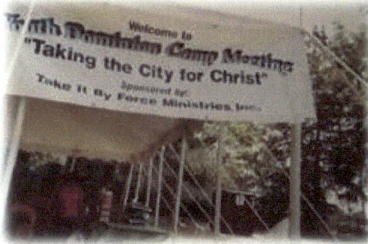

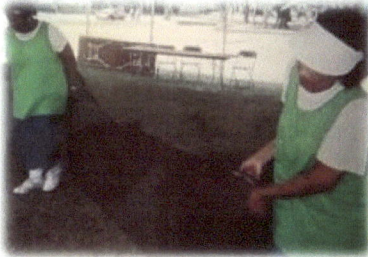

The Heart of an Entrepreneur

A JOURNEY THROUGH TIME

3
Get in the Zone

L et's take a look at something I call the entrepreneurial prayer zone. The entrepreneurial prayer zone is a place where the **problem**/need/imbalance (**disequilibrium**) and the **solution**/entrepreneur/balance (**equilibrium**) interact with each other. For the entrepreneur, the zone includes a series of ups and downs, which can eventually lead to a new threshold of positive change in the marketplace. The goal is to bring balance to an imbalanced environment. Consider my whiteboard in graphic (1).

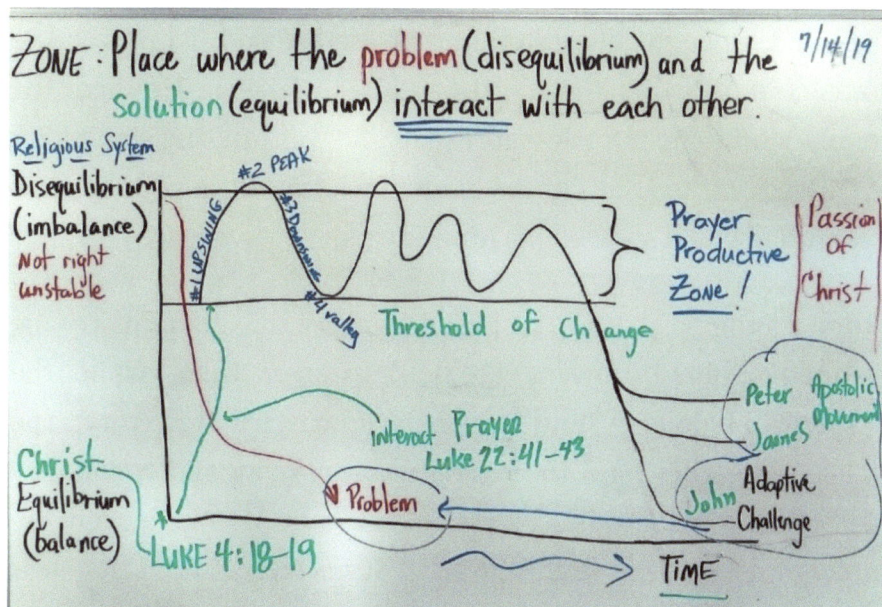

Graphic 1

Initially, in the world of the entrepreneur, the problem/ imbalance is above the solution/balance. For Christ as an entrepreneur, the imbalance was the **religious system** (upper left of the graph). The system was already high and lifted up. But when the balance of **Christ** came onto the scene (lower left of the graph), he took the low road or sometimes what is called the subordinate position. He did not come in on the peak!

Always remember that the low road is simply the beginning point of your upswing moment. You can never be too good to take the subordinate position. Christ took the low road with a sense of: compassion, integrity and humility; when he stated, "The Spirit of the Lord is upon me, because he hath anointed me to preach the gospel to the poor; he hath sent me to heal the brokenhearted, to preach deliverance to the captives, and recovering of sight to the blind, to set at liberty them that are bruised, To preach the acceptable year of the Lord." (Luke 4:18-19). He had the compassion to help the less fortunate, he was offering something of integrity, and he knew under whose authority he was operating, which showed his humility.

From graphic (1), as Christ began to carry out his ministry, he gradually gained upward momentum over time, while the unstable religious system began its downward trajectory. The stakes got higher, and the tension, controversy and conspiracy surrounding his ministry grew, because Jesus challenged the frailty of the system. In Luke 6:6-11, Jesus operated his business in a way that solved the problem and challenged the frail thoughts and intents of the heart. He came into the synagogue on the Sabbath day to teach, but his opponents were watching him to see if he would heal also, so that they could bring an accusation against him. Jesus did not let their intentions hinder him from producing. He healed the man, knowing the conspiracy against him. The religious establishment could not take it and immediately sought a plan to bring Jesus down (v. 11).

Business for Christ was a roller coaster ride. As he approached crucifixion, he prayed to his father in Luke 22; showing reservation about what was to come; nevertheless, he understood that he was entering into the meat of the assignment, the productive zone. The emotional and physical stress was getting ready to intensify, ultimately concluding with his death: only to have the hope of mankind arise with his resurrection.

As an entrepreneur, you should understand that: **never** should **the less**er will prevail; but the greater will should be done (v. 42). Your will represents the "lesser." God's will represents the "greater." For Christ as an entrepreneur, what emerged as a result of his suffering and resurrection, was a threshold of change that would benefit all of humanity while ushering in the Apostolic movement: a movement that would help establish the new covenant order of Jeremiah 31:33 and the early church.

Organize, manage and carry the risk of your solution into the marketplace, knowing that you will encounter a roller coaster ride along the way: it's called the productive zone. But it's good to know that Jesus encountered his own roller coaster experience as a testimony that you can get the job done and have a positive impact on the lives of others.

****Heart 2♡! –*When TIBF sponsored a local middle school, I volunteered to serve as the PTA President during a time when the position was vacant. I had been serving as a fatherhood involvement coordinator for six years and was interested in leading the PTA efforts at the school, even though I did not have a child attending the school at the time. Now this was a huge leap out of my comfort zone and I had my reservations. But it is good to think outside of the box. That is why I included an open box icon on the back cover of this book. The possibilities are endless when you have an openness to learning. It gets the mental gears going towards questioning the status quo while ushering in new ideas.*

I thought the President position would be a good fit, because I had leadership experience along with the passion to see parents involved. Parental involvement was something I had to learn. Earlier in my parenting, I allowed my work schedule to be an obstacle in my involvement. But, eventually I realized that my kids only grew up once, and I needed to be involved. So based upon my own personal struggle, I knew I could be a witness to other parents.

I found myself in the bottom left corner of the PTA zone! My goal was to usher in a threshold of change that would include a student leadership and creative writing initiative. It was a roller coaster ride, where all eyes were on me to see how an African American man would perform in a role that was traditionally held by a woman. I knew God had given me the vision for the hour, and I had to step outside of my "lesser" introvert self; and allow his "greater" will to be done! During my two-year tenure:

I overcame several attempts to replace me, inspired my board members to achieve greatness, served as a student mentor, implemented a successful initiative, and enhanced my networking and social media design skills! The keys to my success were: compassion, integrity and humility. You can't beat them!

20th Camp Meeting Event

August 8, 2009

2010-2013 Camp Meeting Events

25th Camp Meeting Event

August 9, 2014

2015-2018 Camp Meeting Events

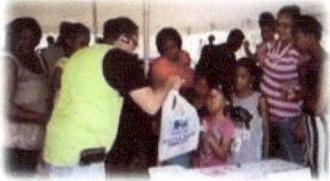

The Heart of an Entrepreneur

A JOURNEY THROUGH TIME

4
Let's Break it Down

Let's dig a little deeper into the word entrepreneurship. There are 4 components I want to bring to the table. The first component is **ENTRE**. When you look up the word entrée in the dictionary, there are two definitions that are relevant to the ministry of Christ as the ultimate entrepreneur.

The first definition is **freedom**. In John 10: (15,17-18), Jesus understood that no man would take his life. Because of the knowledge he had of the Father, he knew he had been empowered to freely give his life as well as receive it right back at the resurrection. The beauty of being an entrepreneur is the freedom you have to run your business! You're basically working for yourself, and that is a wonderful thing. Jesus said, "I and my Father are one." (John 10:30). Jesus was, in essence, working for himself, as an entrepreneur does, but he understood he was accountable to his father. He and the father were on the same page, and his will matched the father's will.

The second definition is **meat** or the **main course** of a meal. It's why you come to the table. Jesus testified in John 4:34, "My meat is to do the will of him that sent me, and to finish his work." He understood what his main course was and had an appetite for it. Know what your meat is. Know why you come to the table! For me, I come to the table to empower youth and young adults to become responsible model citizens. That is my entre, meat and main course in life!

Now let's take a look at the next component, **PRE.** This is where **pre**paration comes in. Being a successful entrepreneur takes a lot of prep work. Mentally, you must be teachable. Jesus said in John 8:28, ".. I do nothing of myself; but as my Father hath taught me, I speak these things." In his humanity, Christ demonstrates the importance of being able to receive instruction from God. It also illustrates a certain level of humility and dependence upon God to help. Earlier in John 5:30, he said, "I can of mine own self do nothing: as I hear, I judge: and my judgment is just; because I seek not mine own will, but the will of the Father which hath sent me." A willingness to listen to Godly instruction can be very beneficial when you are an entrepreneur. Especially when the unexpected occurs.

One morning in John 8:1-11, Jesus was teaching in the temple when the religious leaders brought an adulterous woman before him. They asked him what should be done to the woman, hoping he would give them an answer that they could use against him (v. 6). He did not immediately respond to the question but was silent long enough to confer with his father about what would be the appropriate response to the situation. The response Jesus gave in (v. 7) **defused** the plot to entrap him while **offering** a moment of self-reflection to those accusers who were challenged in their own lifestyle choices. Entrepreneurs must be prepared to defuse and offer. Defuse the problem and offer a solution.

Along with preparation comes the necessity to shadow someone who is doing something similar to what your passion is. For me, that person was a local pastor in my hometown. For the disciples, it was Jesus. Shadowing is very beneficial because it prepares with hands-on experiences that will help you down the road. Having the opportunity to serve as a Youth Pastor was instrumental in conditioning my heart and mind to serve young people.

******Heart 2**♡! – *Over the years, I have learned how to recognize relationships in the marketplace as being seasonal. Seasonal relationships are used to help enhance your knowledge base and fine-tune your vision. These relationships bring added value to the table without the hassle of a lot of strings attached. In other words, you get what you need and move on! Resist the tendency to embark upon every single cause, association and social media group. Be selective in your networking, and don't overwhelm yourself with a list of ten thousand things to do! Know the difference between good things and right things. You can engage yourself in a lot of good things, but are they the right things? Good things deal with what's morally correct. Right things deal with what's moral and necessary at that time in history—doing the right things maximize time. You seize what's in front of you for the greatest benefit. Everything else can wait!*

Just ask Mary and Martha when Jesus came to visit (Luke 10:38-42). Martha was concerned about a lot of good things, but Mary decided this stuff can wait! It will be here tomorrow, but it's time for me to sit down with Jesus RIGHT now! Sometimes we need to have a Mary moment and chill out!

****My ⬆️Turn! - Are there any seasonal relationships in the marketplace that you have made permanent? Are they really needful? List them here along with the advantages and disadvantages of each.

_____

_____

_____

_____

_____

_____

_____

_____

_____

_____

_____

_____

_____

_____

The third component I want to mention is **NEUR**. Neur(o) deals with the nervous system. You must have the nerves (power, endurance and control) to release a useful product that will meet the needs of the marketplace. Oftentimes for Jesus, he entered environments that were filled with jealousy and conspiracy. Some of the religious leaders were jealous of him because he functioned with the power and authority they did not have. Jesus did not allow their opinions to hinder him from delivering the goods! He had the nerves to execute his market strategy. He healed when he saw the need (Luke 13:10-17) regardless of what day it was; and forgave sins (Mark 2:5) when he deemed it necessary. In both episodes, he faced criticism from his opponents; but had the nerves to release his ministry in the marketplace!

Do you have the nerves to execute your market strategy and release the idea God has given to you? There must come a point in life where you are willing to help those in need even if it offends some and causes you a little anxiety. It's part of carrying your cross.

****Heart 2♡! – *I remember when I wrote my first book, Spirituality & Sexuality A Godly Perspective. Because it is a crazy world out there where any and everything goes, I knew the book would strike a nerve, based upon some of the content. The book did not contain anything vulgar, but it did touch on topics that an individual may struggle with and not feel comfortable talking about. However, I understood if the subject is in the Bible, then there must be an honest attempt to present it from God's perspective. In my years of being a youth, working with youth, and being the father of three children, I knew that God had given me the assignment of writing the book to reach those individuals who needed help in those areas of life. As an entrepreneur, it was an opportunity to step out there and release what God had given to me, not only in book form but also in a personal growth workshop, which are great tools for youth and young adult groups!*

So, the last component I want to discuss is **SHIP.** A ship is simply a vessel that is used to transport people or cargo. But for our purposes, it also transports ideas! As an entrepreneur, you serve as an **earthen vessel** or **ship** just loaded with ideas and commodities such as: books, workshops, initiatives and other beneficial material that the marketplace needs. For some, the commodities are still in mental or draft form. Now is the time to identify your port of call, doc your ship and unload: which means you have got to get moving. Go ahead and: write the book, facilitate the workshop, and launch the Podcast. Leverage your ideas!

In Matthew 10:1-8, Jesus downloads the commodity of power unto his disciples and gives them a port of call along with the itinerary for the journey. He tells them what they can expect and how to respond accordingly (vv. 9-22). He was basically giving them the blueprint for the ministry that would occur in the book of Acts. It was up to them to follow through on the assignment.

Being an entrepreneur is ministry: helping others. Helping others begins with an idea or plan. Soon, it becomes a treasure, or something of value in the marketplace. It must be understood that there is a certain way to navigate your ship and distribute that value. The Apostle Paul does a great job outlaying this protocol in 2Corinthians 4. First of all, the **word of God** should help determine the value of what you offer by: renouncing all dishonesty, craftiness and deceitfulness. In other words, don't' be slick or greasy (v. 2).

Secondly, let the **Gospel** shine through your operation. Don't be timid in allowing the mind of Christ to become an integral part of your processes. Your entrepreneurial efforts should be as if Christ was doing it himself, and reflect the **image of God** in the earth (vv. 3-4). Thirdly, your business should be a testimony of how the Lord helped you through your own struggle, thus causing you to approach the entrepreneur endeavor with a sense of humility and servitude to Christ (v. 5). Fourthly, modeling after Christ in the business arena is not a sign of weakness but shows you can put the **knowledge** of God's word into relevant practice (v. 6). Your business should be a beacon of light in a marketplace that is filled with darkness. Does your line of business bring light or perpetuate darkness?

Lastly, in regards to the **SHIP**, there should be something of value on the inside of you that God wants to share with the world for HIS glory, not yours (v.7). The ministry of Christ was based on doing what was pleasing to the Father. Reputation was not a priority for Christ as an entrepreneur. According to Philippians 2:7, "He made himself of no reputation..." Jesus was: meek, lowly, and successful in connecting with his audience.

****Heart 2♡! – *It's amazing how God enabled us to leverage the camp meeting concept into an outreach vehicle that offers: leadership, creative writing, life skills training and other personal growth workshops along with the SWATEENS summer camp initiative. It is truly a ship full of opportunities. The greatest challenge is advertising and collaborating with like-minded entities to deliver the goods! That's a good challenge to have!*

****My Turn! – Have you ever been nervous about a product that you had to offer? What contributed to the nervousness and were you able to launch it? If launched, reflect upon the success story. If not launched, are you going to try again? Why or why not?

30th Camp Meeting Event

August 10, 2019

31st Camp Meeting Event

ZOOM ✠ MEETING '20

For HIS GLORY

Mime MINISTRY

PRAISE
&
WORSHIP

August 27, 2020

Leadership Initiative

Creative Writing

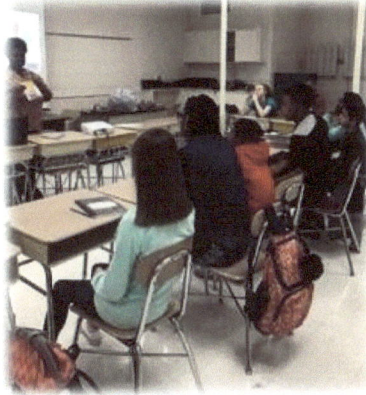

Life Skills Training

S.W.A.✝E.E.N.S.™
YOUTH EMPOWERMENT CAMP

The Heart of an Entrepreneur

A JOURNEY THROUGH TIME

5

The True Heart

L et's get to the heart of the matter. The heart is a hollow organ that maintains blood circulation. When something is hollow, it has a certain level of unfilled space within. The challenge in life, is that there is always something competing to fill your heart. Proverbs 19:21 says, "There are many devices in a man's heart..." Many devices include thoughts and intentions that compete for a space in your heart. As an entrepreneur it is easy to allow the nature of competition and wealth to dominate the walls of your heart, while trying to establish your business in the marketplace. However, life does not consist in the abundance of material possessions and titles; but rather in seeking God's righteousness.

According to Jeremiah 31:33, "... After those days, saith the Lord, I will put my law in their inward parts, and write it in their hearts; and will be their God, and they shall be my people." This scripture shares God's plan for the new covenant of salvation; ushered in by Jesus Christ. The goal is to impact the heart. God's desire is that you would allow his word to dwell within your heart, that you may bring forth good treasure. Good treasure in the form of: love, joy, peace, longsuffering, gentleness, goodness, faith, meekness and temperance (Galatians 5: 22-23).

As an entrepreneur for twenty years, I have learned that there are three things essential to the heart: Compassion, Integrity and Humility. I truly believe that these were key ingredients in the ministry of Christ; that enabled him to be so effective. The challenge in business is not to sacrifice those three components for the sake of profitability and brand. Each component should have a space at the boardroom table.

Compassion is the ability to identify the problem coupled with the intent to: **eliminate** the problem, **reduce** the impact of the problem, or **give strength** to endure the problem. Jesus showed compassion on these levels in John 5:8-9 (He immediately eliminated the man's physical issue), John 8:9 (He reduced the tension in the room by excusing the accusers that made the woman's situation worse) and Acts 1:6-8 (The people wanted restoration, but Jesus assured them of strength from the Holy Ghost instead).

As an entrepreneur, it's not always about your ship's capacity to hold or accumulate; but rather, what is your ship's compassion towards: eliminating the problem (provide employment to an unemployed individual), reducing the impact of the problem (provide temporary shelter for the homeless) or giving strength to endure the problem (mentor a youth who may not have a father).

Integrity is the ability to do right when no one else is around. If you are going to be in business like Christ, then you have got to have some integrity. Paul hits this nail on the head in 2Corinthians 4:1-2. I talked about this scripture in the previous chapter. Don't be greasy!

Humility keeps you from getting the big head especially when you are riding that upswing curve towards the peak! Remain humble in your entrepreneurial journey. Be thankful for the opportunity to serve in such a capacity. Learn how to pray like Solomon (1Kings 3:9) and model after Christ (Philippians 2:5-8). When Solomon became king, he didn't know what to do. He needed the Lord's help. Sometimes when we don't know, it humbles us. Approach God; being an entrepreneur in need of an understanding heart that can serve the people and discern between ethical and unethical. Seek his will for your business and do your best to make it happen! That's what Christ did!

****My Turn! —In each heart chamber below, list how you have shown that component of the heart. Do you have an area you would like to improve upon? If so make a note in that area and ask the Lord to help you.

Compassion

Integrity

Humility

Our world needs a Godly revival; especially among our youth. Homicide is the third leading cause of death for young people ages 10-24. Each day, about 13 young people are victims of homicide and about 1,100 are treated in emergency departments for nonfatal assault-related injuries. While the extent and types of youth violence vary across communities and demographic groups, youth violence negatively impacts youth in all communities—urban, suburban, rural, and tribal. It starts with the core of the individual: the heart. TIBF is excited about addressing this issue through its T.I.M.E. leadership initiative. The initiative emphasizes to the participants that their life matters and it starts with having a heart of: compassion, integrity and humility.

January 11, 2021, marked the 20th anniversary of TIBF. Over the years, I have learned the true meaning of servanthood: it's the sincere desire to help those in need without sacrificing the quality of the product being offered.

Whatever your goals are in life, keep Christ first and foremost, allowing his example as an entrepreneur to be your roadmap towards a rewarding business and life adventure that will serve others and bring God the glory!

But the Lord said unto Samuel, "Look not on his countenance, or on the height of his stature;... for the Lord seeth not as man seeth; for man looketh on the outward appearance, but the Lord looketh on the heart." (1Samuel 16:7)

2020 and Beyond

TIBF Marketplace ENTREPRENEURSHIP

Compassion · Integrity · Humility
T.I.M.E.

LEADERSHIP ACADEMY

Sponsored by:
Take It By Force Ministries, Inc.
Wendell, NC

Takeitbyforce.net

The Heart of an Entrepreneur
A JOURNEY THROUGH TIME

KELVIN K. LUCAS

Leadership Training for Teens &Adults

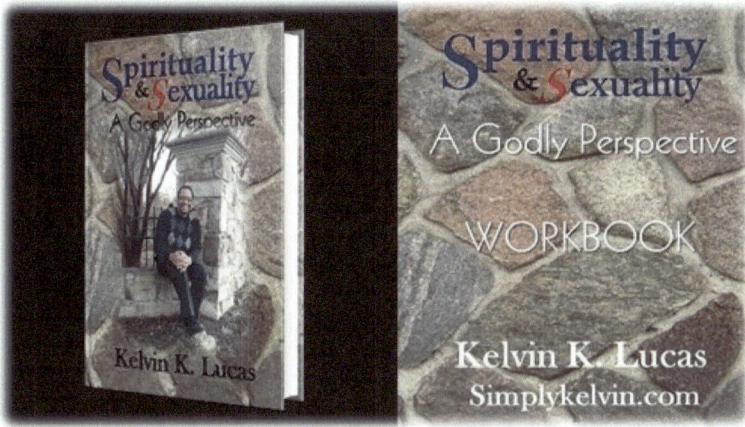

Personal Growth Workshop
for Teens & Young Adults

The Centers for Disease Control and Prevention suggest that young people aged 15–24 years acquire half of all new STDs in the U.S. and that one in four sexually-active adolescents has an STD, such as chlamydia or human papillomavirus (HPV). Compared with older adults, sexually-active adolescents aged 15–19 years and young adults aged 20–24 years are at higher risk of acquiring STDs.

Time is of the essence and God is challenging us regarding the importance of moral living. If you're a youth leader looking for a practical personal growth workshop for teens and young adults, reach out to us at Takeitbyforce.net!

Pro*life* Initiative

Since the 1973 Roe v. Wade Supreme Court decision, over fifty-four million babies have been aborted in centers around the nation. Of that number, more than 19 million of those babies were African American. Abortion is the number one killer in the African American community.

This initiative is designed to take a stand for the most vulnerable of all: the *unborn*. To learn more contact us at Takeitbyforce.net!

"And whoso shall receive one such little child in my name receiveth me." Matthew 18:5

ABOUT THE AUTHOR

Pastor Kelvin K. Lucas- husband, father and Leadership Coach- grew up in Rocky Mount, NC. As a student attending Rocky Mount Senior High School, his journey towards servanthood began when he obtained his first job at the age of 16 at a local retail store. From that time, he began to embark upon learning a trade that has spanned for over 25 years and has taught him the essential key to empowerment...SERVING.

After receiving a B.A. Degree in Business Management from N.C. State University, Pastor Lucas took his trade to the next level by accepting a corporate executive position with a major retailer. Through those years, he learned the leadership dimensions that would transition him into the next season of his life.

He was ordained as an Elder in July 1999, and in 2001 co-founded Take it By Force Ministries, a 501© (3) organization that offers community outreach events, leadership, creative writing, and life skills training for youth and young adults (www.takeitbyforce.net). In 2018, he released his first book, Spiritualty & Sexuality A Godly Perspective.

Pastor Lucas truly understands the meaning of servanthood and has taken that passion to the community as a recreational sports coach, parent leader within the educational system and mentor within the community at large.

He and his wife, Felicia, have been married since 1997, have three wonderful children, and are the Pastors of Dominion Tabernacle in Rocky Mount, NC.

Notes

Notes

Contact Information

Website: www.simplykelvin.com

Facebook: Simply Kelvin Lucas

Instagram: Simplykelvinlucas

Twitter: @Simplyklucas

simplykelvin.com

His Glory Creations Publishing, LLC is an International Christian Book Publishing Company, which helps launch the creative works of new, aspiring and seasoned authors across the globe, through stories that are inspirational, empowering, life-changing or educational in nature, including poetry, journals, fiction and non-fiction.

DESIRE TO KNOW MORE?

Contact Information:
CEO/Founder: Felicia C. Lucas
www.hisglorycreationspublishing.com
Email: hgcpublishingllc@gmail.com
Phone: 919-679-1706